THE SMART LAWYER'S EMAIL PLAYBOOK

TIPS, TRICKS, AND PRACTICAL ADVICE FOR CAN'T-MISS LAW FIRM NEWSLETTERS

Charley Mann & Jenny Sajdera

CO-FOUNDERS OF
RED KRAKEN CREATIVE

CONTENTS

INTRODUCTION

Over the last decade, I've pressed send on at least 2,000 broadcast emails. Frankly, that's a conservative estimate. After all, there are over eight years of near-daily emails, so we're looking at 2,000 to 2,500 right there. Plus, these days I write emails for two companies (Law Firm Alchemy and Red Kraken Creative), and my email sending history goes back nearly 15 years.

I've seen how powerful email can be when it's used properly.

Many years ago, I started advocating for law firms to use the platform more often. Not just in automated sequences, but for regular, frequent communication. To me it seemed like a no-brainer, with your email list a ready-made method of building your "know, like, and trust" factor.

What struck me was how few law firms actually embraced it. Most avoided sending emails altogether, worried about being ignored, unsubscribed from, or worse, seen as a nuisance.

Even with law firms I coached through my other company, Law Firm Alchemy, email was sporadic and undercooked. Firms would send the occasional "newsletter," such as a quarterly or monthly email filled with updates, all of which sounded more like corporate press releases than actual communication. I started encouraging them to do something different: send a weekly email that wasn't a newsletter at all, but instead a simple, straightforward personal message.

For those who followed the formula, the results were almost immediate.

Coaching clients started telling me:

> "I'm actually getting replies."

> "I landed a client from this."

> "A referral partner just asked me to coffee after reading my email."

> "People actually left us new reviews on Google after I asked them in the email."

It became clear that this kind of regular communication was a missing piece for most firms. But there was still a problem. Writing and sending an email every week takes time, focus, and consistency.

That's when my friend Jenny Sajdera and I began to look for a way forward.

We asked: Could another company handle this for law firms at the level it needed to be done? We searched, but what we found was disappointing. Most "email services" were tacked on as side offerings, with generic copy-and-paste newsletters sent monthly or quarterly. Even those who claimed to send weekly emails weren't following the right processes to ensure they were delivered, opened, and acted on.

Eventually, the conclusion was obvious: if no one else was willing to do it right, we would have to build it ourselves. Jenny and I had already talked about starting a business together, and this was the perfect opportunity. We knew what was missing, we knew how it should be done, and we knew the market needed it. We founded Red Kraken Creative together, and have made it our mission to inform and serve law firms looking to gain a competitive edge by using the tools they already own.

That's where this book begins. The lessons inside come from years of testing, coaching, and building a business around doing email marketing the right way. My hope is that by the time you finish, you'll see email not as something to avoid, but as one of the simplest, most powerful methods of growing your business.

—**Charley Mann**
Co-Founder
RED KRAKEN CREATIVE

EMAIL MATTERS

It's a Very Noisy World Out There.

Let's start by stating the obvious. It's a loud loud loud loud world, and we're just living in it. Even our pets are involved/annoyed.

Social media in particular generates so much noise, as do the latest streaming services, podcasts, YouTube videos of those podcasts being recorded, and more, that it's hard to hear your own voice, let alone broadcast it to a larger audience audience. Attached to nearly all of these noise-generating mechanisms are the algorithms—those unseen but not always unnoticed beasts that ensure we're fed an endless supply of whatever it thinks we'll like. The technology is so adaptive, and so persistent, that a single click on a reel about dressing your cat for Halloween can have you fending off videos featuring Princess Purr-fect and her latest formal attire for months on end.

Which is to say, the traditional, practically monolithic media landscape most of us grew up on has been overrun by innumerable streams, reels, shorts, tiks, toks, and more—all of them created to obtain the most precious of commodities these days: Attention.

With each passing day, the channels we have access to seem to get noisier and noisier. Advertising in this environment is less like shouting into the void, and more like screaming at the bottom of the ocean.

All of this is why email matters.

Despite the complaints of overflowing inboxes, people still pay pretty close attention to their emails.

Email isn't swiped away like a TikTok video, nor do the algorithmic overlords have control over how many people see your subject line like they do on LinkedIn. Deliverability is high. And, when done right, so is consumption.

If that weren't convincing enough, email is also the world's #1 marketing channel with Campaign Monitor finding "email marketing produces an average of 174% more conversions than social media." Obviously, we have our biases.

We're an email marketing company. But the data, and the practicality associated with email, speak for themselves.

Red Kraken Creative was built with the express purpose of helping others—folks just like you—build their own vibrant and profitable marketing ecosystem, with email as the foundation. We handle your email newsletter from start to finish, every week, for as many months as you'll have us.

We love email for its reliability, versatility, adaptability, and scalability. What other marketing tool can simultaneously:

- Protect you against the whims of algorithm updates from uncaring social media companies
- Give you a direct line of communication to your audience, allowing you to get a timely message to everyone who follows you
- Scale in a way that's practically infinite with nearly zero cost
- Drive traffic to your YouTube content to generate the initial views that help accelerate growth on the platform
- Isolate your reader's attention on your message, while insulating it from the interruptions or urges to skip/scroll you would have to contend with on social channels

- Create a built-in model for future segmentation so you can send specific messaging to smaller subsets of your audience (again, without worrying about the algorithms)
- Make it easy to stay in front of everyone who contacts you
- Drive new reviews to your law firm
- Connect you to referral sources with high frequency and consistency, keeping you top of mind for future referrals

Email is a community bulletin board, editorial column, promotional postcard, and breaking news alert rolled into a distribution model your audience checks in with multiple times per day. Not even direct mail can compete with the level of earned attention email garners.

There are countless more nuanced opportunities in email marketing as well, but the ones above encompass the core of what we help clients accomplish at Red Kraken Creative.

However, unlike the Norse sailors whose ships met a horrible fate at the hands of the mighty squid creature known as the Kraken in their ancient mythology, this Kraken is here to help.
Ready to get started? Great. We're here to help. We

want to give you the tools you'll need to write better emails—to stop screaming into a sea of noise—and give you the power to bellow from the depths like an ancient, eldritch cephalopod.

This is our playbook.

Why would do give it all away? Because we honestly believe email-based marketing is so simple, nearly anyone can do it.

It's effective. It's impactful. It's got the highest ROI of any marketing channel you could hope to leverage on your behalf. **But it's not easy.**

There are technical details you need squared away, strategies to follow to ensure maximum deliverability, open rate monitoring, templates to build, clicks to track, lists to curate and grow, and reply campaigns to create so you're not just sending emails, you're building a vibrant, engaged, healthy community.

Oh, and of course there's the writing and the sending and the replying and the strategizing about what to write the next week and the one after that. Did we mention you'll need to send out at least one email per week to get the results you're likely hoping to achieve?

Like we told you, email isn't easy.

And anyone who tells you to drop any slapdash slop into the digital marketing realm should be tried at the Hague for international marketing crimes.

This is the Red Kraken Creative email marketing playbook. It won't be the biggest book on your shelf, but it could be the most impactful, especially if you commit to both following our process and understanding the philosophy behind why we do what we do.

This playbook is everything you need to start your law firm's email newsletter. From verifying your DKIM, decluttering your list, writing killer, compelling subject lines, or building review campaigns that generate results, we're not just sharing the recipe for our secret sauce, we're giving you a bottle of the good stuff on the house.

What you do with it is up to you.

And should you find the heart is willing but you're running out of the limbs required to plan, prep, and execute a powerful email strategy, well—we've got a few extra tentacles we'd be happy to put to work on your behalf.

Now, on to the playbook...

THE FOUR THINGS YOU NEED TO DO

Five, if You Count Reading This Book

We said it before, but we're saying it again here (and will probably say it again half a dozen more times, like a mantra):

Email is simple. But email is not easy.

The recipe for a great email newsletter has just four components. Like cooking a great steak, while the ingredients might be minimal, it's easy to end up with an underwhelming, criminally under-seasoned dish or an over-salted slab of inedible char if you aren't careful (or, in some cases, refuse to take any risks).

Here are the four things you want make sure you get right for every email:

1. Get it delivered.

2. Get it opened.

3. Get it read.

4. Get it acted on.

In our experience, marketers are generally comfortable with items 2 & 3 on the list. That's not to say they're good at those things, only to say that's what they've put most of their time and energy into learning how to do. In some cases they even do it well. Which means that the real magic is in the bookends—1 & 4. Getting it delivered, and getting it acted on.

The middle parts are in most marketers' wheelhouses. Comfortable. Maybe even fun.

Write great subject lines and punch out some great content for the reader, and boom. The hard part's over. Or so they think.

Spoiler Alert for Future Chapters: While most marketers think they're nailing subject lines and are adept at crafting clear, compelling copy, the truth is most people are doing these parts wrong. More on this later.

We can't emphasize enough how important it is to learn and implement all four of these.

Don't pick and choose. You need to do all of it.

If your email isn't delivered, it can never be opened.

If it isn't opened, it's not read.

If it's not read, no one acts on it.

And if no one is acting on it, then what's the point?

Let's solve for all four components.

GETTING IT DELIVERED

AKA All the Clunky, Chunky Tech Stuff.

Your email's journey from your brain and into your audience's inboxes relies on a series of systems, each with its own crunchy little acronym:

SPF.
DKIM.
DMARC.

You need to know those little jumbles of letters to succeed with email marketing, because they are the backbone of email health. They gained notoriety in February 2024 when Gmail and Yahoo started to require DKIM and DMARC for emails to reach their users. This move caused quite a panic, because every move the tech companies make freaks people out. But overall this was a positive change. It helped get some of the bad actors out of the email marketing scene.

The shortest way to describe what these acronyms do is by saying: **They tell email programs you are the actual owner of the domain, and that you approve of the email system sending messages on your behalf.**

As a trio, they affect whether your emails reach your list, protect your reputation, and keep you compliant with rising standards in cybersecurity.

Here's what each record does, and what your firm needs to know:

1. SPF (Sender Policy Framework)

This says who is allowed to send email on behalf of your domain.

Your SPF is a lot like a naval registry. It lists all the ships (servers) officially sanctioned to carry your flag. Any vessel not listed on the registry is viewed as a fraud or pirate ship and turned away at port (your audience's inboxes). The SPF checks the sender's IP address against a list of "approved" senders (like your email provider, CRM, or case management system).

If the sender isn't on the list?

They're denied entry or marked suspicious.

What law firms should do:

- Make sure your domain's SPF record includes all the services you use to send email (Gmail, Outlook, Clio, Mailchimp, etc.)
- Don't just trust your IT company to get this right. Ask for confirmation of your SPF record and cross-check it with your vendors.

2. DKIM (DomainKeys Identified Mail)

DKIM is like putting the captain's wax seal on all communications. It doesn't just say "this came from me," it says "this came from me and wasn't tampered with along the way." Your unique DKIM marks your emails with a cryptographic signature to prove they weren't altered in transit.

What law firms should do:

- Ensure your email platform (like Google Workspace or Microsoft 365) has DKIM signing enabled
- Note: This isn't always "on by default"—ask your IT or vendor to confirm DKIM is configured and signing messages correctly

3. DMARC (Domain-based Message Authentication, Reporting, and Conformance)

Think of DMARC as the admiral's standing orders with regard to any scalawags that may be trying to sneak into port under your banner without authorization. Should their ships be sunk on sight (reject), held up for further inspection (quarantine), or simply noted in a log for the captain to review at a later date (none/report)? If an email fails an SPF and/or DKIM check, your DMARC setup tells receiving mail servers how to handle it. It is arguably the least important of these three tools, but it's the third leg on the stool. How you use it is up to you.

What law firms should do:

- Set up a DMARC record that starts in "monitoring" mode (p=none) to gather intel
- Once you're confident SPF and DKIM are properly configured, move to a stronger policy (p=quarantine or p=reject) to actively block fraud

So, for the sake of review:

SPF says who can send.

DKIM says the message is legit.

DMARC tells servers what to do if something smells fishy.

And together, they stop email spoofing cold—protecting your clients, your cases, and your credibility.

Feeling Overwhelmed?

Maybe you saw a few consonants in a row, or maybe you hate nautical metaphors. Either way, you've barely read 20 pages and still said, "I'm out on this." We get it. This aspect of email marketing isn't hard to set up, but it has to be set up the right way. Otherwise, your emails will go straight to spam. Most modern ESPs (that's email service providers, if you're not into the whole brevity thing) give you direct instructions on how to set up your SPF, DKIM, and DMARC.

But if you want to skip the hassle, you should know that RKC takes care of this process for our clients. The most stress you'll have is locating your logins or putting us in touch with your web providers.

Oh, speaking of ESPs...

YOU NEED AN EMAIL SERVICE PROVIDER, BUT WHICH ONE IS BEST?

The type of email newsletter we recommend sending requires you to bulk-send broadcast emails. It may seem obvious, but there's a difference between the personal email you use to share cool photos of your dog with your family and the the platforms you'd want to wield if you wanted to send the same photo to 5,000+ people (please include us!).

It's the difference between a canoe and a steamliner. Could you use a canoe to get 5,000 people across the Atlantic? Technically yes, if you don't mind taking multiple trips. But the journey will be fraught, and will likely take at least 10,000 times as long. When you want to send a bulk email, it's best to use a vessel built expressly for that purpose.

There are some client management systems (CMSs) for law firms that include email marketing functions. However, they may not have the best sender reputation. This matters quite a bit. Sender reputation is sort of like a referral relationship. When someone keeps sending terrible leads your way, eventually you're going to start ignoring their calls. Sure, 1 in 10,000 of the folks they send your way might be a meaningful connection, but the work required to sort through the dreck is rarely worth the effort.

Likewise, if the platform you're using allows a lot of shady actors to send spam emails, when your message shows up via the same platform, user inboxes are going to scrutinize it:

"Is this message worth the risk?"

"Is it another one of those unseemly phishermen? Or perhaps a down on his luck Nigerian prince?"

"Probably safer to kick it to the spam folder."

So into the spam folder it goes. Even if you don't belong there. And that's not where you want to be.

You can avoid all this by using one of the more reputable ESPs. These days, most email service providers (ESPs) are also customer relationship management (CRM) tools. You can send emails while also putting people through automated sequences, keeping notes about them like a spy agency, and also segment them through something usually called "tags." We'll talk more about those later.

We are often asked which email sender is the best.

We could give you the "it depends" answer. That would be the truth.

But then you might get angry and throw this book into the sea. Or a pond. Or just across the room, cursing the Kraken's good name. And you're only 1/4 of the way through the vital intel here, and water has a tendency to make books harder to read. So we'll capitulate and say that, in general, we do have a few favorites, with two de facto front-runners.

But the ESP that's right for you depends on what your priorities are. **Our default recommendations for point-and-shoot, ease-of-use bulk email blasts are ActiveCampaign and MailChimp.**

The primary reasons are because the programs connect with darn near everything, and we have several clients who use them successfully.

Other platforms worth considering are Kit (previously ConvertKit), as well as MailerLite, and Omnisend.

You could go insane trying to pick the perfect one.

If you want a full-scale CRM system with email attached to it, Hubspot, Go High Level, and Salesforce are great options. Red Kraken Creative currently uses Go High Level as our all-in-one CRM, ESP, and sales pipeline tool. That said, when you use one of these larger CRMs, they may route you through a bolted-on email service. Technically, our emails are sent through Mailgun, though all of the setup is done in our GHL account.

See, we told you this is a lot of technical stuff. All of it just to send an email.

But it's worth it.

Once you properly set up your ESP, you have this incredible tool of communication at your fingertips.

Push through the pain (or hire us to take care of it), and you'll be glad you went through the effort.

Once you nail it, your emails will land in the inboxes of every member on your list.

From there it's just a question of whether or not they'll read it. If only there were a way to ensure the answer to that question is nearly always yes...

GETTING IT OPENED

On the Subject of Subject Lines

Now that you've nailed getting your email sent to each member of your list and have done the front-end technical work to ensure it lands in their inbox as opposed to their spam folder, the next step is to give it a chance to capture (and hold) your reader's interest.

To continue with the nautical metaphors we've been tossing around, you've made it to the ocean and you know where you want to fish. But to ensure you go home with a prized catch or two, you gotta bait the hook. The bait you'll choose is determined by dozens of factors.

Though experienced fishermen might disagree on what's best for which fish, all will tell you an unbaited hook is a waste of time—as is fishing in an area where thousands of other boats have dropped anchor and line.

The same is true for email, but unfortunately, there's no way to change the fact that every reader's inbox is lousy with eager fishermen, hoping their lines will catch the attention of their prize. And since you can't change that fact, it's important to control the one thing you can: **You have to have superior bait.**

That means every email needs a captivating subject line— the sort that simply begs to be opened. While there's no guarantee you'll hook a trophy fish (aka qualified lead) every time you cast a line, you can get yourself quite a few nibbles (aka opened emails) if you use the right bait. Open rate isn't exactly the gold standard for whether or not an email should be considered "good," (especially for law firms!) but it's a useful metric to track because at the end of the day, if it's high that means folks are at least engaging with what you've created and if it's at zero there's something disastrously wrong with your messaging (or the means you used to send it).

This begs the question, "Well then what's a good open rate?"

Before we give a number, let's get into the seaweeds about what an open rate can tell you, and what it can't. While it's tempting to chase a magic number, the reality is that open rates vary dramatically from firm to firm, list to list, and even month to month. What works for a solo practitioner in a small town is going to look wildly different from a midsize firm in a metro area.

Why? Because open rates are influenced by factors beyond your control—email platforms that block tracking pixels, spam filters that bury messages, and recipients who preview your email without technically opening it.

Of course, different subject lines can have different impact as well. Again, different bait for different fish.

That's why the smartest strategy is to stop obsessing over isolated numbers and start focusing on trends.

- Are your open rates generally rising or falling over time?

- Did a particular type of content spark more engagement than usual?

- Are certain segments of your list more responsive than others?

These patterns tell a much more useful story.

Doing some monitoring on your newsletter's open rate should be about progress, not perfection. Think of it as a compass, not a stopwatch. It points you in the right direction, but it doesn't tell the whole story.

Now, we still promised you a number. Let's deliver on the promise.

We wouldn't want our open rate to be less than around 17%.

And if it's higher than 60%, you should probably be more aggressive about adding names to your list. Yes, it's a wide range, but as we stated, the most important information is the trend. Don't panic just because you pressed send and only got 12% open rate. This just means your list likely needs some cleaning, and there may be deliverability issues to address. The data tells a story, and we can adapt our strategy according to the story we see.

One way to do that? By using the best bait we can find for the fish we want to catch. That starts with creating an excellent subject line.

COPYWRITING TO MAKE THEM OPEN THE EMAIL

In our world, there are two types of subject lines.

1. Repeated and reliable

2. Curiosity drivers

Most law firms will benefit from picking one and stick with it, which means you want to determine which style is right for you and your objectives. Each has its advantages and disadvantages.

Repeated and Reliable

We use this setup for Red Kraken Creative with our Founders Letter and Roundup email every week. Why? Because it builds long-term trust with the audience through clarity and consistency.

Our first ever Founders Letter had the following subject line:

"Founders' Letter 1: Preamble and Launch"

This structure repeats every week.

Founders' Letter 2: Stop waiting to use your resources
Founders' Letter 5: The rocket ship feeling

It will always be "Founders' Letter #: Quick Teaser."

We aren't going to get fancy with the teaser. It's not built as a full-on curiosity driver, because we don't want people to only open out of curiosity. We want them opening because of the trust we've built with them.

No gimmicks, no tricks, just consistency and clarity. Over time, it becomes a hook that baits itself.

Sounds good right? So good you're ready to sign off. We don't blame you.

But before you do, take a look behind door number 2. Because you won't *believe* what marketing pros are saying about this **one simple trick that changes EVERYTHING.**

And what you just read is an example of it in action.

Curiosity Drivers

This second subject line style is about teasing the reader with what might be inside.

What outrageous, interesting, or emotionally resonant material hides within the walls of your email? What secret knowledge or unbelievable tale are you about to share? It's like a magazine cover line. You only have 3-10 words to get someone interested. Use them wisely.

The curiosity driver approach has the disadvantage of needing to be refreshed every week. You can't just copy and paste last week's subject line and swap in a simple phrase like "The Latest" or, "Wills and Won'ts," or "Summer's Here!" You have to come up with something new every time.

For some firm owners, this alone adds an extra 15 minutes to the process, most of it spent agonizing over which words are hookier and which lines are more enticing and whether or not it's too late to switch to the Repeatable and Reliable method. That said, this approach has numerous advantages.

Curiosity drivers have a high ceiling on open rates. When you create a really powerful one, you can spike your open rates.

One of the most powerful subject lines for the attention-grabbing experts at *Buzzfeed* was "How to Survive a Zombie Apocalypse." According to BuzzFeed's subject line A/B testing team, these absurd, curiosity-spiking titles routinely delivered 20–30% higher open rates, especially when paired with fun, list-based content.

Now, you may not have a zombie apocalypse disaster preparedness checklist to share, but there are elements of your practice that can be pretty sensational when reframed to pique curiosity rather than directly inform.

People are far more curious about the law than most lawyers believe them to be. John Grisham didn't sell 300 million books because people love pelicans or rain.

What your law firm does is run of the mill...to you. To others? It's the subject of the latest trending documentary or breakout streaming series. Every client and every case has a story, each with an emotional core and its own twists and turns. It's likely that the stuff most folks would find compelling is old hat to you.

But it's not to them. Which means you get to write about stuff you know so well you're bored with it to an audience that's clamoring for precisely that type of content. What's not to love?

You're used to the insurance company putting up a fight against someone who obviously deserves the money. You're well-versed in the lengths some family members will go to deny a brother or a grandson what a dying relative expressly willed him to have. You know what happens when estates get stuck in probate, or end-of-life documents aren't tidied up, or how something as simple as taking out the trash can be disastrous to your personal injury case.

Lawyers know these things because they talk about them all the time, swapping them like fish stories or cautionary tales. But for the general public, things you take for granted are often novel, occasionally jaw dropping, and in many cases truly enraging.

Anyone who studies human behavior in the digital era will tell you that the material that's emotionally resonant is the stuff that drives clicks.

A marketing director at a law firm that uses curiosity drivers told us that the approach comes with baked in ups and downs as far as open rate goes, and their emails live between 29-60% (not for nothing, most firms would be happy with that floor on opens, so she's doing something right). Her best subject lines seem to fall into two categories. Either they are of the moment (e.g. "What you should really know about AI") or relate to a dramatic, emotionally engaging aspect of a practice area (e.g., "What Elon Musk has planned for your Social Security number").

Another famous curiosity driver came from the Obama fundraising team during the run-up to the 2012 election. It was just one word: "Hey"

You see the genius, don't you?

In a world of clever headlines, sometimes the least clever one stands out. There's actually a place for this strategy with law firm newsletters, but you need to tread carefully. Getting cute can get you in trust jail with your audience. More about this shortly.

I actually tested this email strategy, and it worked to get a bunch of opens. However, it didn't do much in clicks or sales. Your mileage may vary.

Again: Expert fishermen will argue about the best bait to use to catch the same type of fish. What you need to decide is why you're choosing bread over worms, and that starts with understanding who/what you're trying to catch. We can help with both.

You also need to know when to cut bait and try something different. We can help there too.

MAKE SURE THERE'S A PAYOFF

The one crime you don't want to commit is having a great subject without content to back it up.

Say it with me: No gimmicks.

You can't send the world's greatest teaser only for the content to be the written equivalent of a deflated balloon. We're in favor of a light dose of sensationalism in your subject lines, but that's just to draw the open.

You never want to "Well, technically" the body copy in your email into a compelling subject line. After all, lawyers already get a bad rap because of a few word weasels who know how to leverage the power of fine print. You don't want your subject lines to further solidify that stereotype.

When Ramit Sethi sends an email with the subject line "Your 7-figure blueprint is inside," he's prepared to meet the interest with expertise. If you opened it up and found some rambling diatribe about a cheap financial product, you might be turned off.

You also don't want your readers to skim the email seeking the answer to a question posed or the payoff to a promise made in the subject line. You want to aim for a quick payoff, as well as clear alignment between the subject line and the text inside. Be careful about doing too much windup before getting to the good parts, aka, the reason they opened in the first place.

If your headline is "Brad Pitt shows you how to hire the right people for your law firm," you'd better have a payoff as soon as they open.

Note: That's an actual headline Charley wrote for a Law Firm Alchemy email. As soon as someone opened the email, they saw the following:

"One of my favorites movies of the 2010s is *Moneyball*, the Brad Pitt-starring film about data changing the world of baseball.

Ultimately...

Moneyball is a movie about finding talent."

The premise of the email was to promote the Catalyst program, and tied directly to its upcoming session covering hiring. The tie-in started in the subject line, using a pop culture reference to draw folks in. As a general note, we're always going to stand by using pop culture to capture attention.

Why talk about yourself when you can talk about Brad Pitt, right?

So how do you start? The good news is the stronger your writing in the body copy of your email, the easier it is to create successful subject lines.

WHEN IN DOUBT, LOOK TO THE MIDDLE

Most writers will tell you beginning a story is often the most difficult part. How to begin! An email's subject line feels like the logical place to start, especially in personal correspondence because that's the line our cursors default to.

But writing a solid subject line is heavy work. You often know what you want to write about, but not always how best to frame it. You typically know what you want to cover, but not necessarily how you want to ramp up to it.

For this reason, the middle of your email is often the strongest part. You're in your element, writing about the stuff you know cold, and because you don't have to worry as much about "What" to write, your mind is better at executing the "How."

And because the middle portion of your email is often the best, it also makes for the best place to cultivate a quality subject line.

What's the weird statistic you highlighted?

What was the inciting incident or sudden swerve in the story you're sharing? How could you frame it as a teaser?

To borrow from pop culture again, many quality filmmakers use a hook format known as *in media res*.

In media res is Latin for "in the middle of things," and that's exactly how this technique works. Instead of starting at the beginning, the story drops the audience right into the action, often at a critical or climactic moment. The backstory and context come later, revealed through flashbacks, character dialogue, or gradual exposition.

The TV show *Breaking Bad* often employed this technique, showing you a short scene of something odd, like a smoldering teddy bear floating in a pool. Quentin Tarantino's career is practically built on dropping you into the action before bouncing around in time so you can see how the pieces fit together. But whether you're talking about Walter White or Mr. White, the goal of the in media res approach is to lure the audience into sticking around for the payoff.

The motion picture industry lives and dies on its ability to hook people and make them stick around. It's harder than ever these days with all the streaming services at our fingertips. Why not steal from the folks who are master's at attention-grabbing and plot-hooking?

And then, once you have the hook in them, it's time to make them read the darn thing...

GETTING IT READ

How to Write Better Emails

Admit it. You skipped ahead to this part, didn't you? It was probably Charley's rants about the power of black text on a white background that drove you to leap to this page. We get it. If we're being honest, this is probably the chapter of the playbook you came for, and is likely the one you'll refer back to most often.

Because if there's one question we get most often, it's this: what the heck goes in my emails?

There are plenty of marketing gurus who espouse the age old premise of "creating value." But we have a bone to pick with this phrase. It's not wrongheaded, per se, but it lacks a bit of context, and is based on a word that is ultimately subjective. What does value mean, exactly? And to whom?

If an email "adds value" but is never opened and read, does it become a falling tree in an empty forest?

Some marketers will suggest creating an email that nurtures, rather than leverages, your relationship with those on your list. That's a secondary form of value. After all, the more you build out that relationship, the more you scratch their back, the more likely it is that they'll help you out (e.g., "Please leave a review!" or "Vote for me for local attorney of the year!" or "Pass along my name to anyone planning a divorce!").

An example of a nurture email is sending a brand new lead a list of 15 ways they can DIY their case with no call to action. Sure, you're creating value, but you're also overwhelming them with information. And the worst part is not having the call to action. We'll talk more about that later.

I'll also share a secret with you: many of the nurture emails I've done in the past have gotten more unsubscribes than standard messaging or emails with specific offers baked in. Again, value is subjective.

It's a tough balance—too much marketing copy and you come off as desperate or trying to sell something. At the least you might stop to sound like yourself. But emails where you sound like yourself might not achieve your goals for this type of communication with any of your potential clients.

So what's the answer?

To simplify, your job is to get the email opened, read, and acted upon. Stick to that metric. Because that's of value to you.

Ultimately, any additional value we can add for the reader is a bonus.

But who doesn't love a bonus?

Therefore, to us, **the best emails are those that get opened and read AND can add value for your reader.**

To create dual value with your email newsletter, we recommend thinking through what value means to you in the short and long term. And to us, a meaningful client relationship is far more valuable than a random single lead. If you agree, keep reading. If you don't, well...keep doing you!

Our approach is to create content that is valuable to you in the short and long term and useful to your clients whenever they need it. It isn't going to be a bunch of free legal information, although it can occasionally take that form (especially when that form can lead to an increase in potential open rates, as might be the case when a high profile trial is dominating the news).

More often, our format suggests creating value through:

- Entertainment

- Novelty

- Superiority

- Connection

These four categories are massive value drivers for your email readers. Entertainment alone is a woefully underrated part of marketing. In a world of bland marketing, the ability to entertain becomes a superpower. Perhaps you've heard of infotainment and/or edutainment. Each of those portmanteaus aims to connect the drab world of teaching with the vibrancy and levity entertainment can provide. The most famous example of this was/is *The Daily Show with Jon Stewart*, which revolutionized the merging of hard-hitting political journalism with gut-busting comedy.

Prior to Stewart, however, cable news channels started to use Superiority and Connection as their primary messaging strategies.

Know your audience, cater to their idea of the world, give them a place where they belong, and make sure they feel correct about their worldview. No sense in challenging them. Give them what they want and how they want it.

While this approach has had diminishing returns for accuracy and journalistic integrity, it's an unparalleled recipe for growth, and explains the rise of podcasts and TikTok as some of the most dominant forms of media today. We're not saying you need to become a talking head spouting conspiracy theories or hawking supplements 24/7, but you should at the least examine why the approach works and what you can take from it.

The simplest way to apply the tricks used by late night hosts and podcast stars is to add a little showmanship to your writing.

Many law firm owners are pretty stellar writers. They are often gifted at persuasion through the lens of a well-reasoned and researched legal case, and bring a sense of flair when delivering their arguments in the courtroom.

Some even weave in pop culture references and familiar anecdotes or relatable metaphors to improve the impact and stickiness of their statements. But for many lawyers, even the great ones, there's a gap between those talents and translating them to a different media format, which is why most revert back to "just the facts, please."

Their writing loses the character and flair that's easily observable in the conference room or courtroom. This can often create resentment of some marketing media formats. Lawyers who are otherwise powerful personalities don't see the same punch in their marketing copy, don't feel as connected to the material they write about themselves as they do the things they create for their clients. So they get frustrated, or get discouraged, or get bored, and they bail.

It's hard to build new habits. It's also hard to do new things, which can sometimes bring a bit of anxiety. Even fear. After all, what will others think if you use the wrong word, or share something too personal, or quote your favorite film and no one has ever heard of it. It's another lonely, falling tree.

But there's a remarkable shift that happens when you see your ideas written out by someone else.

You may experience a shocked sense of delight.

Your ideas are no longer shackled by trepidation or self-doubt, or the hang-ups that might prevent you from breaking the mold in the name of a great story or joke. A writer building on your ideas simply writes, free from the blocks that keep great concepts from coming to fruition.

It's still you, it's your idea, it's your content. It's just being delivered through a more reliable (and perhaps less busy) medium.

That's the service we provide at Red Kraken Creative. But if you're committed to writing your own emails, then commit to studying copywriting greats to understand their rhythms and approach. We highly recommend:

- Gary Halbert

- Stefan Georgi

- Kim Krause-Schwalm

- Dan Kennedy

- John Caples

- Parris Lampropoulos

These true masters of direct response copy never left the body of their copy to chance.

All killer, no filler between the headline and the close. Every line was considered part of the overall experience. Once someone was "in the copy," these writers knew they had to keep them there, line after line, sentence after sentence, until the reader either begged for the offer or couldn't scroll fast enough to click on the ol' order button.

What separated their body copy from the amateurs was how deliberately they designed every word to do one thing: keep people emotionally and psychologically engaged every step of the way.

For email, we want them utterly engrossed or instantly eager to see what is at the bottom for them to act on.

I'm not saying you need to figure out how to become the next copywriting great. But you should do what you can to learn from them.

It's a high standard to keep. But worth the effort. And since we're in the game of raising your standards, here are a few tricks the pros use...

Give the Text Surprises in Structure

Great copywriters understand that the real enemy you're facing is never the competition. It's boredom. If a prospect's attention drifted, the sale is lost. The masters mentioned earlier knew this through instinct and experience, and eventually created what is now described as "the greased slide," a narrative structure and practically audible rhythm that made it nearly impossible for the audience to stop reading.

The approach starts with short sentences that break expectations.

One-liners.

Quick punches.

Maybe a joke about a hippo.

Then, *bam* you drop a longer paragraph that shifts the tone, builds intensity, and raises the stakes. You aren't just writing to inform; you're writing to arouse curiosity, stir emotion, and provoke action. Every sentence becomes a little promise: "Keep reading, and I'll show you something you didn't know before."

Be Conversational

What makes the greased slide approach work so well is the copy deployed always feels like you're part of a conversation, not a lecture. Halbert famously imagined himself talking to a friend at a bar with a cocktail napkin in one hand, pen in the other.

His goal wasn't to sound smart. It was to sound real. He anticipated objections mid-stream and answered them before they could bubble up in the reader's mind. He layered in stories, often gritty, specific, sometimes outrageous tales that mirrored the reader's pain or nightmares, hopes or dreams.

The idea of copy rhythm and conversation go hand in hand. Most conversations are not a series of three sentence calls and responses.

When we talk, we create declarations, run-on sentences, quick fragment responses, and other structural choices that, in the written form would drive a grammarian insane.

But they keep people engaged.

That's why the copy greats work wasn't just read. It was devoured.

They didn't write to inform. They wrote to move. And once you were in, there was no turning back.

This probably feels like an impossible standard.

After all, you have a weekly email to write, and you're not chasing down punches on the "buy now" button.

But why not learn the good stuff?

I think of it like dialing in a golf swing. You wouldn't learn the bad version of it. You want to learn the proper technique (though Bryson DeChambeau may challenge that orthodoxy) so you have the best odds of success as you build reps and strength.

YOUR WRITING MINDSET

Here's a bit of free golf advice that also translates to email: The biggest shift you need to make is often between the ears.

All the tactics and tools are worthless if you're not in the right mindset. If you're tense or afraid to go for it. I can see it all the time in the public text from lawyers I work with. On the phone and in person, they tell incredible stories and know how to keep your attention locked in during a conversation.

But if you put them in front of a keyboard, the dynamic personality evaporates. They lock up, as if an invisible Catholic nun school teacher with a yardstick is about to come by and rap their knuckles if they have any fun.

And it's not just the emails. They do it with social media posts and video scripts. The fun and character and personality is gone.

So whatever you do, be yourself. Let it flow. Don't think so much about what to write, think instead about what you want to say. Why you want to say it. Lean on your expertise, but also the aspects of your personality that people most readily associate with you (or that you keep to yourself because you don't want your clients to know you're also a Level 16 Orc Paladin closing in on Tiamat's lair in your years-long Dungeons & Dragons campaign).

If you love SEC football, work in a few sports metaphors.

If you're an aspiring gourmand, ask yourself how the premise you want to talk about could tie back to a technique you use (or know to avoid) in the kitchen.

If you can't think of what you want to say, think about something you saw recently that made you say "Man, that's messed up/very cool/totally off-the-wall," then consider what your audience might be interested to learn about the legal side of things.

Are you a film buff? Analyze one of your favorite scenes from a legal perspective: "Yes, as a matter of fact, Marisa Tomei did deserve the Oscar for *My Cousin Vinny* because not only was her accent on point, but she also convinced a fictional jury she was an automotive expert. Here's why that wouldn't work in real life..."

Writing about things you care about is as simple as telling a great story to your friends or family.

But there's that word again. Simple, not easy.

Especially if you're planning to do so once a week for the foreseeable future.

Luckily, there's a solution. We've mentioned it before, but we'll say it again: If you're feeling overwhelmed by the prospect of creating a custom, personal email newsletter that sounds like you and adds value to your customers through the form of consistent connection and reliable, top-of-mind visibility, **we want to help.**

A BIT ABOUT EMAIL DESIGN

You're busy. And ready to start writing your emails. You don't want to read an entire chapter on what it should look like, and we've got great news: You don't have to.

Black text.

Plain white background.

That's all you need to succeed with email.

In fact, in our opinion, it's pretty much all you'll want. If you stray too far from the core identity of what email is/ has always been, you lose a lot of the potency that makes it effective. Remember, your email is not an Instagram post or flashy magazine.

It is a direct communication with your audience.

You don't run a fashion brand or car dealership. Visuals are not core to what you deliver, nor are they necessary to build a strong relationship with your recipients.

Keep it simple.

Black text. White background. Maybe, *maybe*, some blue hyperlinks and a letterhead-style logo.

There are a few reasons we focus on just the text in email newsletters:

- **Variety = visibility.** Most email marketers are now trying to get clever about their design, meaning your "plain" emails will actually stand out for most consumers.

- **Images impact deliverability.** They remain a risk factor for carrying malicious links, and with mass distribution the gatekeepers grow concerned the images could be, well, let's just say provocative. While we do expect AI will help with the latter issue over time, there's no reason to add the extra risk of a bounce back or of landing in spam land if you don't have to.

- **Most folks are on mobile.** Many people check emails on their phones. However, broadcast emails are written and set up on a computer. The design elements may not translate as expected, if at all, when shrunk down to the mobile size.

- **Clean = clear.** Why distract the reader from the main message with all manner of wanton design elements or funky fonts? Clarity is king.

We aren't saying NO NO NO to images in general, especially if you're all-in. Additionally, there may be times when it's appropriate to add a photo or graphic. And if you want to add one, well...that's your right.

An image or two every now and again isn't going to be the end of the world, or suddenly shift your bounce rate.

What we do worry about are the emails that are jam-packed with images and chockfull of graphic elements, including:

- Header logo

- Author photo

- Bottom of email firm logo

- Stock photo

- Thumbnail for a video

- An image of your new kitchen sink from your recent remodel

You don't win at email by making it slick, pretty, or, fiercely slay. Even one of my favorite graphic designers, Kia Arian, keeps her emails clean and uncluttered by images.

Make the text your "design element."

Take a look at the way this book is written, or how any of the emails from RKC are constructed. The text is treated as an image. It's built to keep the flow moving. You don't need every paragraph to be three lines. You can keep a reader's attention by mixing things up.

You can also keep their attention by throwing in a little surprise every now and again.

If you watched our free training video on email (nab it at *redkrakencreative.com/guide* if you haven't already), we go into great detail about all of this, and share a few examples of great writers to learn from.

All of them create rhythm with their text.

So break it up!

Use single lines and fragments.

Don't be afraid to bend and even break the rules of grammar. Full stop.

People read text by speaking it out loud in their minds. This is why writing in a conversational tone has so much power. You are in a dialogue with the spoken voice in your reader's head, chatting with it rather than sharing the full text of your thesis.

You're not publishing a *New Yorker* article. If anything you'd be better off sharing a *New Yorker* cartoon. But, like we said, avoid images, so...

In general, our overall rule about images is that you get no more than two.

Some firm owners want the law firm logo at the top of each email. This makes sense for firms that have a growing brand presence, or those who want to link together all of their marketing efforts under the same visual signifier. Totally get it. But a logo counts as one image. And everything you add after that starts to build deliverability risk.

Now, you may wonder why you have to pay attention to the images when other brands use them willy-nilly.

First off, you're not out here to look like every other brand. It's Marketing 101: Show up different. And you can be different by keeping your marketing emails as text-focused as possible.

Second, the domain and sender reputation of a massive brand is greater than yours. They don't need to pull out all the stops to avoid being tucked away in spam. You might.

Third, many big brands just accept a wider margin of error. You shouldn't.

TEXT IS A BUNCH OF IMAGES

Ultimately, the text you use is a series of images people turn into words in their minds. The real caretaking needed is for the text itself. Earlier, I mentioned you should use black text on a white background. I must hammer this point home.

Black text. Full black.

Not blue. Not dark gray. Not off-black.

Black.

Gray text in particular is an infuriating recent phenomenon. We've seen countless websites for law firms where the words practically slip off the screen because of the lack of contrast.

Max out black text.

On a white background.

Don't get fancy with your email's background. You're not sending an email from your free Constant Contact account in 2007, so the big bold color used as the wrap around your email body is no good. Remember, many people will see your email on a mobile device, meaning the fancy border color won't really show up. It's just one more design choice drawing away from the main text.

Black text.

White background.

Max out contrast.

We've seen plenty of counterarguments from the design community. "But the aesthetic!" "You calm the mind before you speak!" "More is more, and more is good!"

We love designers. But they are wrong.

We are unyielding in this decision. It's got to be black text on a white background, the same way it would appear as a plain text email.

There is some debate on whether or not you can or should use emojis in emails. We're not against using them in email. But we typically don't.

An Australian email marketer, Daniel Throssell, uses them regularly. Our guidance here is: If emojis are endemic to the way you communicate online, work them in. Otherwise, don't think you're creating a magical advantage by incorporating them into your emails.

The more you focus on the text, the better your overall results will be.

Let's circle back to our design friends for a second, who are still a little mad and pose a question that comes up quite a bit (and that we will answer in a way that might also make them mad): What font should you use?

Standard practices suggest a sans serif font. To anyone who isn't a typography designer, a serif font is one where the letters have little fancy bits and bobs around them. Those bits and bobs are called serifs, and the typeface we've used here (and throughout most of this book) is a serif font.

> This font doesn't have any serifs. It is "without" or "sans" those little bits and bobs. It is therefore referred to as a sans serif font.

The most common serif fonts are: Times New Roman, Georgia (this font), Garamond, and Palatino.

The most common sans serif fonts are: Arial, Helvetica, Futura, and Roboto.

We recommend Times New Roman, Georgia, Arial, or Helvetica for email. They are common, comfy, and play well across all platforms.

If you want to choose something different, all we can say is don't get too fancy with your choice. With apologies to the design department, there's simply no need to forge your own path here.

The next part of the equation is size.

For us, 14 point is the minimum. Emails from Red Kraken Creative are usually set up with 16 point font, because it is easy to read thanks to its size. We find the grade school essay standard size of 12 point font too small for digital devices, and even on much larger computer screens.

Is that more information about fonts than you ever wanted to know? Probably.

Here's one more request, especially for those who grew up learning to type on older word processors: **Do not use a double space after a period.**

We see this less often these days, but there are some who cling to this old-school typesetting rule until they leave this mortal plane. Modern word processing software made the need to create a little space between a period and the start of a new sentence automatic long ago, which means any time you add a second spacebar keystroke you're making that gap too big.

Stop. Please. Stop.

See how spacey that is?

It looks better like this:

We. Are. Begging. You.

BEWARE THE UNFORCED ERROR BY USING TEMPLATES

There can be a lot of strange spacing errors in your emails due to paragraph and line spacing decisions. Just send yourself several test emails and dial in your design.Then, save the design as a template.

Templates are your friend. You don't want to keep setting up the design elements of your emails every time you open your ESP. Spend the time up front to get it right, then reuse it over and over again.

GETTING IT ACTED ON

Calling All Calls to Action

The vast majority of firms fail at the first part of email marketing. As you no doubt recall, the first item was the technical side, all the deliverability details, with those lovely acronyms: SPF, DKIM, and DMARC.

But many also fall short on the fourth component, which also has a cool acronym: CTA.

A CTA, or "call to action," is what separates the serious marketers from the "just getting my name out there" crowd.

A CTA is your invitation to the reader to do something. Whether it's "Book Your Consultation," "Download Our

Free Guide," or "REPLY to this email," the purpose remains the same: to move someone forward.

Or, perhaps more simply, to move them.

A great CTA does more than ask.

It directs.

It clarifies. It builds momentum.

Think of your marketing like a well-built sports car. Your headline, your copy, your presentation—every part can be top of the line, fine-tuned and tested for maximum performance. But if there's no CTA, the car doesn't take anyone anywhere. It just sits in the garage.

What separates good CTAs from great ones is clarity combined with purpose. Generic phrases like "Click Here" or "Learn More" might check the box, but they don't always spark action. The CTAs that convert say something with meaning and urgency. They tells people what they're getting and why they need it right now.

This doesn't mean every email ends with some outlandish promise with a deadline-driven call to action.

For most firms, we recommend using an email newsletter for long-term relationship building.

Your CTAs will often drive readers to:

- Watch a video on your YouTube channel

- Reply to enter a giveaway

- Leave new Google Reviews

- Check out an article you wrote or a story you found interesting and worth sharing

- Grab a free resource

And yes, there are times when you can and should focus on case referrals. Newsletters sent to professional contacts will lean on the referral language frequently.

But all of this is predicated on one idea: You ask, they answer. You say "Would you mind," and they say "Well, of course not!" But you don't get what you don't ask for.

That's why we flip the script. We don't ask them, we want them to ask you.

At their core, the best CTAs answer a question your audience is asking, even if they don't realize it: "What should I do now?" If you haven't provided an answer to that question, they'll move on. But you answer it with strength, specificity, and value, they'll take action. And that's how marketing creates results.

So here's the real takeaway: if you want your message to move people, you can't end it with silence.

End it with direction. End it with purpose.

End it with a CTA that's impossible to ignore.

WHAT DOES A CTA LOOK LIKE?

Despite what some reports may have indicated some time ago, there is no combination of color and button type that will triple the results of your CTA. You're working with a much smaller traffic volume on your email opens than a 9-figure e-commerce business that would conduct such studies. Sure, a red button with white type might lead to a .17 increase in clicks over the course of a three year period, and for a billion-user business that shift means big bucks. But for you it's likely less than one click overall. So don't think big about the small things, think small about the big things. What works? What doesn't? Why/why not?

All most firms will need to include is a link to click.

Or give the reader the direction to "REPLY" to the email.

You don't want this to be complicated.

The design choices you're making here are meant to support the outcome (action), not win design awards. For our clients, this usually means a basic button or blue text link. We choose function over form.

And to add a bit more here, your simplicity can once again buy you some visibility. Most corporate emails are going to have focus-grouped buttons or A-B tested, illustrated image links. You don't want to look like you're sending a corporate email, you want to look like one of your reader's friends or family members.

You're not the latest t-shirt trend or Supergreen supplement. You're a law firm that can help.

Offer that help, and tell them how they can help you, in a way that's aligned visually and verbally with who you want to be: Their neighbor.

PUTTING IT ALL TOGETHER

Like a gumbo, only something you read.

Like all marketing, email newsletters represent challenges and opportunities. They are simple. But they're not easy.

Everyone thinks they can do one, yet so few actually press send. It's easier to just drop something on social media at the end of the day, so they resort to platforms they often resent rather than the one they use every day for team and client communications. Email is a consistent, practically omnipresent part of our lives. It is the modern equivalent of direct mail and faxes rolled into one, a means to send a message directly to your audience's pocket or purse. This is what makes it so effective. It's also what makes it such a popular marketing method.

The advantage you have over your competitors in this space is your ability to keep pressing send—to face down the moments when you think you just don't have the next email idea in you and figure it out. Charley wants every law firm he works with to use a weekly email newsletter as part of their marketing slate. It's not the first thing he prescribes to the firms he works with via Law Firm Alchemy, his coaching business, but it shows up very, very early as part of our overall referral marketing gameplan.

The primary plays outlined in the plan are: weekly meet-ups, a monthly mailer, and (drumroll please) a weekly email broadcast. We know email marketing works because we've been preaching it for years, and have seen huge results for those who listen to our guidance and execute.

Remember, you need to do four things with your email:

1. Get it delivered.

2. Get it opened.

3. Get it read.

4. Get it acted on.

The whole game is in those four concepts.

Start with the technical part. It's the foundation on which everything else is built. Yes, it has those gnarly technical details you need to set up, but you can overcome those (or let us take care of it for you as part of handling your email newsletter in full).

Then, think about what you want email to do for you. Let's bring Stephen Covey's *7 Habits of Highly Effective People* into the mix here and "begin with the end in mind." What do you want your emails to achieve; what goals can and will it achieve for you?

Once the platform is ready and you know what you want from it, the creative work can begin. And we've landed on why email fails for many. They start from wanting to be creative. We do that after we know why we're getting into the game.

In all the marketing you do, creative should start with boundaries. This sound counterintuitive, but guidelines and limits improve creativity overall. Ask any writer what the scariest thing they face each day is and most will tell you "The empty page." When you don't have any idea what you're meant to be writing about, the sheer possibilities can stunt your ability to get started. But tell a writer to give you a few sentences describing a man who is about to ask for a loan to start a business, or is sailing in a harbor, or is about to step out of a spacecraft and onto the surface of a new planet, and they'll spin out sentences that are touching, terrifying, tantalizing.

You don't need to think outside the box. Use the box to help you think. Marketing with the broad goal of just getting attention rarely, if ever, has the same punch as marketing with a more direct purpose. The more specific the objective, the better the creative work turns out. Why do you think most people like the earlier work of music artists, back when all they had were a few chords and basic producing? That's when they had a real story to tell and something they had to get out in the world.

Your email is you putting something out into the world. Know what your goal is, get those technical details right, and start pressing send.

Nothing to it but to do it, right?

DON'T WANT TO DO IT YOURSELF?

OK. Twist our arm. We'll do it.

You studied the full strategy. You learned the technical mechanics of email deliverability, the psychology of subject lines, the copywriting tactics that hold a reader's attention, and the importance of clear, consistent calls to action. Great job.

You now understand what it actually takes to turn email into the most reliable marketing asset in your firm. This is the full playbook.

You're ready to go! Oh wait, you have a client meeting. And after that another one. And then of course there's that deposition you need to review, and the kids have a recital tomorrow morning, which means you'll need to write this week's email...yesterday?

It's simple. It's not easy. Work, life, and your limited, precious, truly valuable time, start to but up against your will to get the job done and what starts as a few weeks in a row of sending quality content becomes a month of saying "I'll get to that next week," which evolves into one email a quarter that mentions a call to action you forgot to embed a link into.

Reading about email isn't the same as writing it. Writing isn't the same as sending. And sending a few emails is a far cry from doing it every single week for the next year. That's why, for all the law firms who say, "We need to be doing email," only a tiny fraction follow through in a meaningful way. And fewer still get the full benefit.

Let's change that...

WHY MOST LAW FIRMS ABANDON EMAIL BEFORE IT PAYS OFF

Over the years, I've seen countless firms start down the email path. They write two or three emails, maybe five if they're determined. Then, life happens. The caseload grows. The team has questions. The marketing calendar gets crowded. Suddenly, that weekly email feels like a luxury.

It stops going out. Or worse, the firm starts feeling guilty for "falling behind" and decides maybe email just isn't for them. The opportunity slips away—not because the strategy doesn't work, but because the execution was never sustainable.

You need more than a strategy. You need a system.

That's where Red Kraken Creative comes in as a done-for-you email newsletter solution that keeps your firm top-of-mind, builds relationships, and drives measurable results like referrals, reviews, and revenue.

WHAT RED KRAKEN CREATIVE ACTUALLY DOES

Let's get specific.

When you work with us, your email newsletter becomes a self-sustaining machine. Our team takes over the process completely—from writing to technical setup to performance monitoring—so your only job is to enjoy the benefits.

And those benefits are as big as the multi-limbed cephalopod we use as our namesake.

By working with us, you'll stay in front of your office on a consistent basis. This audience includes past clients, referral sources, potential leads, and professional peers who think highly of your work but forget to send you business because they haven't heard from you in months. Your name will start showing up in their inbox every week—not as spam, but as a well-crafted letter in a trusted voice that shares useful, relevant content.

You'll drive real, trackable outcomes. That might be new Google reviews, more scheduled consultations, or a steady stream of case referrals.

This is relationship marketing that works.

You'll reclaim your time and mental bandwidth. No more staring at a blinking cursor on Sunday night, wondering what to write. No more Googling "what are some good email subject lines" or tweaking templates from five years ago. You won't have to think about it. We'll handle the writing, the uploading, the scheduling, and the tracking. Your emails will go out every single week on time with purpose and in your voice.

THE RED KRAKEN PROCESS

Let's walk you through what it's actually like to work with us, so you can see how this turns into a true set-it-and-forget-it system.

First, We Get the Tech Right

As you now know as well as you know your own name, email doesn't work if it doesn't get delivered. That's why our team handles all the background setup that most law firms either ignore or don't even know they need.

We configure your SPF, DKIM, and DMARC records to ensure maximum deliverability. As a reminder even though you don't need it because you read and retained everything in this book, these are the "digital signatures" that tell inboxes like Gmail and Outlook that your email is legitimate. Without them, your emails get marked as spam or bounced entirely. We work directly with your web host or IT provider to get this right. You won't have to touch a thing—except maybe sharing a login or two.

Then, We Learn to Write Like You

Your emails should feel personal. That's how you build trust and generate replies. So we don't write in some generic, legal-marketing tone. We build what we call your Creative Dossier.

It's a reference file that captures your personality, tone, preferred stories, and communication style. This dossier guides our writers to sound like you on your best day. Whether you're punchy and bold or warm and thoughtful, your newsletter reflects you, so your audience feels like they're hearing directly from your desk.

We Align Your Email with Your Goals

This is where most newsletters fall short.

They exist. They're sent. But they don't actually support the firm's business objectives.

We don't let that happen. Early in the process, we create your Opportunity Portfolio, a living document outlining what you want your newsletter to achieve. Whether it's more referrals, more reviews, greater YouTube viewership, or increased website traffic, your content is strategically aligned to push those outcomes forward.

You get performance with purpose—not just a "nice" newsletter that makes you feel productive.

We Take Over the Weekly Execution

This is where the magic lives.

We write the email. You approve it. We upload, schedule, and send it for you.

Every week.

No skipped weeks. No rushed last-minute writing sessions. No guilt. We make your newsletter consistent— and that consistency is what turns readers into referrers, past clients into promoters, and contacts into cases.

We Monitor, Optimize, and Improve

Once the system is in motion, we track the performance of every send. That includes:

- Deliverability (our goal is 100%)

- Open rates (we track the trend, not just one-off spikes)

- Click-throughs (who's engaging and what they're clicking)

- Replies and referrals (your real-world ROI)

You'll see the data. We'll review the trends. And we'll evolve your strategy to match what's working. You get clarity, confidence, and continuous improvement without ever needing to guess whether your emails are "doing anything."

THE LONG-TERM BENEFITS

We're not in this to give you short-term marketing sugar highs. We're building durable marketing equity—the kind that pays dividends over years.

Here's what you gain when you hand over your email newsletter to Red Kraken:

- Top-of-mind positioning with everyone in your network

- Reliable referral flow from people who already trust you

- Higher client retention and re-engagement (for repeating practice areas like estate planning)

- More Google reviews and online social proof

- Faster traction on your video and content marketing

- Time returned to you and your team because you're not racking your brains to write the next email

A weekly email newsletter isn't a nice-to-have. It's one of the best media formats to be in front of your clients and referral sources year round.

And it works. Not because of marketing theory, but because it's rooted in trust, consistency, and smart copywriting, delivered with precision and purpose.

WHO WE SERVE (AND HOW WE MAKE IT EASY)

Our clients are growth-minded firms in the legal space—typically small to midsize firms in consumer practice areas like estate planning, family law, immigration, criminal defense, disability, and personal injury. We also work with select B2B firms and business law practices.

Most of our clients already have a list (even if they haven't used it to send anything it in a while), and many have experience working with marketing vendors or internal teams. What they don't have is time. And what they want is leverage—a way to stay visible without being overwhelmed.

That's exactly what we provide.

Our onboarding is simple. You fill out a short application, we schedule a strategy call, and within days we're building your tech setup, your Creative Dossier, as well as your first few emails.

Once we're rolling, your involvement is minimal. Just 30-60 minutes per month to review and approve a month's worth of messaging.

You'll get to watch your email become a high-performance part of your firm's growth with no ongoing time drain.

IT'S TIME TO PRESS SEND

Or Rather, Have Us Press it For You...

You can see the truth. Email works. It escapes the algorithms and gives you a direct line to build relationships with your list.

But it only works if you send it consistently. And for most firm owners, that consistency is the killer. It's what separates the firms who get leads from email and the ones who let their list go stale.

You now know how the system works. You've seen what goes into each part—from technical setup to creative development to strategic alignment.

And now, you've got a choice. You can DIY it. Carve out the time, stay on top of the copywriting, the sending, the analysis, and all the rest of it.

Or...

You can hire Red Kraken Creative and have it all handled for you, week after week, without fail, by a team that eats, sleeps, and breathes law firm email marketing.

Here's how to get started:

→ Visit www.RedKrakenCreative.com

→ Click the "Work With Us" tab

→ Follow the instructions on how to get started

That's it.

From there, we'll walk you through your current situation, help you clarify your email goals, and show you how our team will take the reins. You'll get the playbook turned into a system—one that delivers consistent visibility, engagement, and results.

So, don't let this be just another marketing idea that sounded smart but never took off.

Turn your email newsletter into the smooth-sailing vessel it was always meant to be. Let us press send for you.

ABOUT THE AUTHORS

Charley Mann has worked in, for, with, and on law firms since 2010. And he has sent more than 2,500 email broadcasts for companies he's run and owns. Now, as a co-founder of Red Kraken Creative, he brings those two expertises together to help law firm owners dial in their email marketing to get more clients and develop deeper relationships with the people who follow them.

Jenny Sajdera has worked in operations and marketing since 2008, and has helped launch hundreds of email campaigns for companies she has managed and supported. As a co-founder of Red Kraken Creative, she combines those experiences to help lawyers turn their email newsletters into powerful referral engines.

www.ingramcontent.com/pod-product-compliance
Lightning Source LLC
Chambersburg PA
CBHW070945210326
41520CB00021B/7061